Himalayas
Bottom to Top

Written by Simon

Contents

Collins

Introduction

The Himalayas are the mightiest mountains in the world. Their icy peaks are so cold that we humans must wear special clothing or freeze to death. They are so high up that we must breathe bottled oxygen or we could die. Sometimes called the "Roof of the World", the Himalayas stretch about 2,500 kilometres across the top of India eastwards into China. All of the world's 100 highest peaks are here, snow-capped giants seven kilometres high where conditions are as extreme as in the Antarctic.

CHINA

Karakoram Range

K2 ▲

nga Parbat ▲

H I M A L A Y A S

KISTAN

Tibetan Plateau

▲ Mount Kailash

Hengduan Shan

Annapurna ▲

Everest ▲

Kanchenjunga ▲

Kawa Karpo ▲

NEPAL

BHUTAN

↗ Sikkim

INDIA

BURMA

3

But there's more to this mountain range than rock and snow. There are deep jungle valleys where tigers prowl. There are hillsides where farmers grow rice and tend their herds of sheep and yaks. There are misty pine forests where the flowers look like the ones you might find in your own back garden. This book is about a whole Himalayan mountain from bottom to top – what happens to the **climate**, the vegetation and the wildlife, and how people live their lives at each level going up.

Yaks are huge, shaggy mountain cattle, specially adapted to live in the thin, mountain air of the Himalayas.

People have travelled these mountains for centuries – taking their cattle and sheep up to high grassy meadows when the winter snows melt, carrying goods to trade in the lower valleys and climbing high up to be closer to their gods. Many people today enjoy climbing the mountains for the challenges they pose. Many of the highest peaks were only climbed in the last 70 years. Since then, trekking in the Himalayas has become big business – but it's risky. K2, the second highest peak in the world, is one of the hardest to climb. Only 300 people have made it to the top and 80 have died trying. To reach the summit of a mountain giant like K2 or Mount Everest, climbers need to be fit, well-equipped, skilled at mountaineering – and lucky!

Kawa Karpo peak and Mingyong glacier

The mountain we'll focus on is Kawa Karpo, also known as the "Meili Snow Mountain". At 6,000 metres, it's not the tallest, but it's still high enough to have wind-blasted rock faces permanently white with snow. The gleaming triangular peak of Kawa Karpo towers above the forests and valleys below. Though its lower slopes have been travelled by people for centuries, its summit has never been climbed.

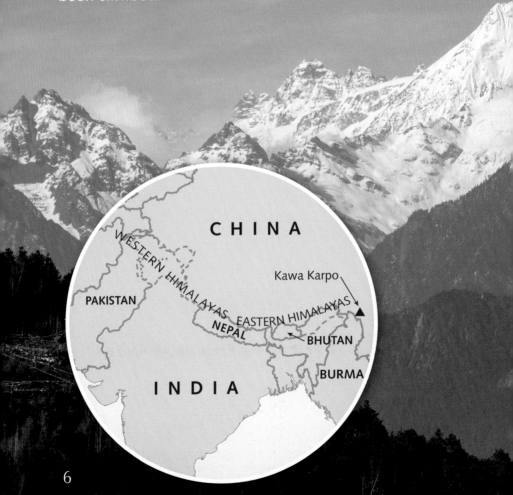

CHINA

WESTERN HIMALAYAS

Kawa Karpo

PAKISTAN

EASTERN HIMALAYAS

NEPAL

BHUTAN

INDIA

BURMA

The mountains of the Eastern Himalayas have a wetter climate than those in the west. The valleys at the foot of Kawa Karpo are warm and almost tropical. The further up you climb, the colder it gets and the thinner the air gets – which means there's less oxygen to breathe. Each level of the mountain has a different climate, each with its own special plants and animals suited to live there.

High Alpine Zone (4,700 metres): High, cold and blasted by the wind, it can be like the Arctic up here, though on the parts of the mountain which aren't drenched by rain and smothered in snow, it can be desert dry. Animals and plants up here have to be hardy.

Low Alpine Zone (3,500 metres): grassy land in summer; snowy in winter

Temperate Zone (1,500 metres): higher and cooler with pine forests and many types of flowering plant that have been introduced to Britain and the rest of Europe because the climate is so similar

Subtropical Zone: warm and wet with flooded fields called paddy fields, where rice is grown, and patches of jungle on the steeper slopes

1000 m --------

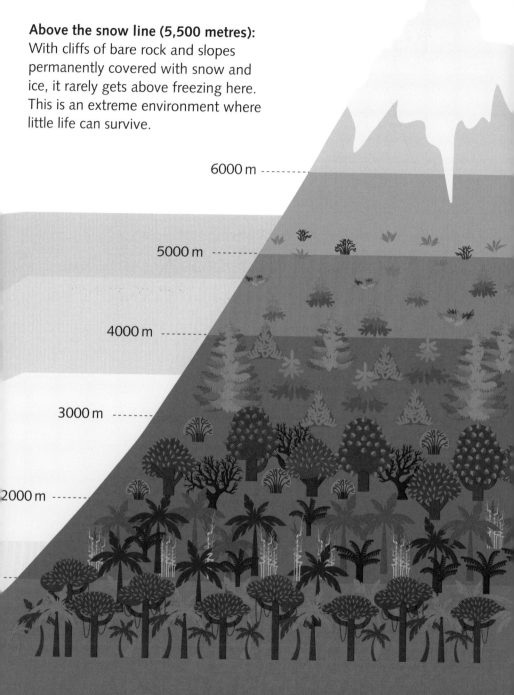

Above the snow line (5,500 metres):
With cliffs of bare rock and slopes permanently covered with snow and ice, it rarely gets above freezing here. This is an extreme environment where little life can survive.

6000 m

5000 m

4000 m

3000 m

2000 m

Subtropical Zone

At the foot of the mountain, the climate is warm and rainy. Every summer, a wind called the "monsoon" blows up from the Indian Ocean, dumping most of the year's rain on the mountain slopes in the space of just three months. It is wettest in July, and the rivers become boiling masses of rapids, coloured brown from the mud washed off the valley sides. When the water levels go down, this mud – and the **nutrients** it contains – is dumped on the land.

The natural vegetation here is evergreen forest, home to metre-long "Giant" squirrels, Macaque monkeys, leopards and Musk deer. Instead of antlers, Musk deer have long fangs sticking down out of their mouths. They also have smelly glands under their bellies which they use to scent mark their territories. These glands are used in Chinese medicine and to make perfume; because of this, they've been badly hunted.

Leeches

The warm, wet forest of the lower valleys is crawling with slimy little worms called leeches. They detect body heat and seek out warm animals and people to attach their sucker mouths on to and drink blood. They're not really dangerous, just unpleasant. Leeches have chemicals in their spit that stops blood clotting so the wounds they make won't stop bleeding. The wounds only start itching once the leech, now fat with blood, has dropped off on to the forest floor to spend the next few weeks digesting its meal.

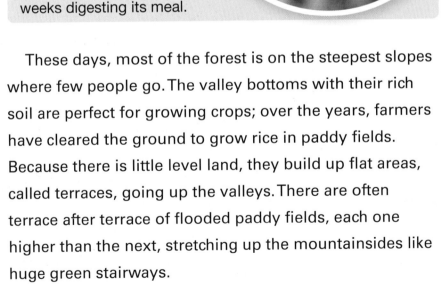

These days, most of the forest is on the steepest slopes where few people go. The valley bottoms with their rich soil are perfect for growing crops; over the years, farmers have cleared the ground to grow rice in paddy fields. Because there is little level land, they build up flat areas, called terraces, going up the valleys. There are often terrace after terrace of flooded paddy fields, each one higher than the next, stretching up the mountainsides like huge green stairways.

As the farms spread upwards, the forest shrinks back. People cut it down to make room for their fields. They use the wood to build their houses and for cooking with. In such a rainy climate, forests soak up water, gradually releasing it into the rivers. Cutting down trees for firewood leaves the bare earth open to being worn away by the rain. Every rainy season, roads, fields and sometimes whole villages are smothered by landslides, when parts of the mountain break off and slide downwards.

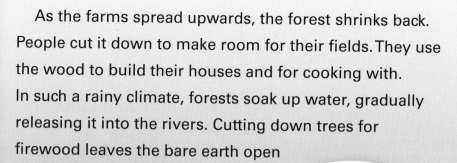

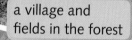

a village and fields in the forest

13

This rainy season happens in the summer across India and much of Asia. The sun heats the Himalayas and the hot air rises. The rising air pulls in monsoon winds from the Indian Ocean and these winds bring clouds full of moisture. When the clouds reach the Himalayas, they are blown up the mountain slopes. As the clouds get higher, the moisture in them gets colder and falls as rain.

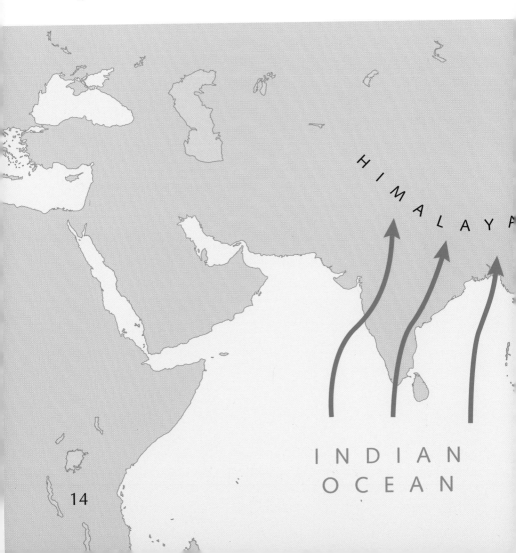

HIMALAYA

INDIAN OCEAN

Rain shadow

While the side of the Himalayas closest to the Indian Ocean is very rainy, the other side of the mountain range is very dry. By the time the monsoon winds get that far, most of the rain that they carried has already fallen. Dry areas like this are said to be in the "rain shadow" of the mountains.

This effect can be seen on Kawa Karpo. The steep valleys, to the south of the mountain, channel the clouds up them and are very rainy and covered in jungle, while the other side of the mountain is dry and scrubby.

heavy rain and snow fall

little rain or snow fall

15

Joseph Rock and the plant hunters

Many European garden flowers come from the Himalayas. There's no accident in that. The climate is similar. Although the Himalayas are nearer to the **equator** than Europe, being high up a mountain lowers the temperature so that the cool, damp climate that they thrive in is similar to a temperate climate such as the UK. Around 100 years ago, it was the fashion for wealthy gardeners to grow the latest, most exotic blooms. To get hold of these, a whole new class of explorer grew up – the plant hunters. Austrian-American Joseph Rock was the "Indiana Jones" of these. He went on his expeditions in the early 1920s. By that time, most of the easy-to-get plants had already been brought back, so his trips took him ever deeper – and higher – into the Himalayas. He travelled to Yunnan in China, a land of deep **gorges** and raging rivers which had to be crossed ... somehow.

At that time in Yunnan, though there were cars and trucks, there was no way they would make it through on the dangerous roads that crossed the mountains. Joseph Rock led his expedition on pack mules, crossing the rivers on zip wires like the local people did. These were made of plaited bamboo tied to thick poles on either side of the valleys. To get across, you sat in a harness made of yak hide; this was looped over the bamboo rope with a wooden slider greased with yak butter. Even the mules and horses had to be strung up and slid across, kicking and bucking all the way. When they reached the other side, they were often too terrified to stand. When he was lucky – and if there were no rapids – Joseph Rock managed to hire dugout canoes.

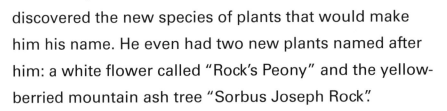

Some of the Lisu people from Tibet helped him. They hunted birds and monkeys with homemade crossbows. Joseph Rock eventually made it up to the high mountain forests and the Alpine Zone where he discovered the new species of plants that would make him his name. He even had two new plants named after him: a white flower called "Rock's Peony" and the yellow-berried mountain ash tree "Sorbus Joseph Rock".

Some of the regions he explored aren't that different today. Transport through the Yunnan mountains is still by mule train, and local people continue to use zip wires to get across a few river gorges, though the main routes now have bridges. The Lisu people are still there and continue to use crossbows to hunt in the forest.

Temperate Zone (1,500 metres)

The temperature lowers up to ten degrees centigrade for every 1,000 metres climbed. The mornings are chilly and it's often misty. Drops of moisture glisten on the clumps of fuzzy **lichen** that dangle off the trees like light-green tinsel. There are tall oak trees here and plants called rhododendrons with pink or purple flowers that attract bees and other insects to **pollinate** them. In the sheltered valleys, these can grow 30 metres tall, though many other types are just undergrowth bushes. The Himalayas near Kawa Karpo are divided by very deep valleys, and each mountain ridge has different species of rhododendrons. This variety is what interested plant hunters like Joseph Rock so much in this region.

lichen

Bamboo is also very common here. It grows well in gaps between trees where sunlight gets in. Where the forest has been cut down by people or blown down by storms, there can be whole hillsides covered in bamboo.

Bamboo is a type of giant grass. There are many species and some of these are the fastest growing plants in the world – they can grow more than a metre in a day! Few animals are able to eat their tough stalks and leaves. The leaves have saw-like edges and contain **crystals** of silica, which is the same substance as sand.

Even though bamboo is so hard to eat, there are some animals which feed on little else. Red pandas have specially adapted **digestive systems** that can break down the leaves and get nutrients out of them. Unlike Giant pandas which live further east in China, they can eat other food too, like small animals, eggs, blossom and berries. Red pandas are active and fast moving, clambering up the bamboo thickets in search of the newest leaves. These are softer and easier to eat.

Sometimes new bamboo shoots are seen being pulled down into the ground. They are being attacked from below by Bamboo rats. These rodents burrow tunnels under the forest, sniffing out the freshest roots then pulling them under to feast on them. This way they don't need to venture above ground and can avoid **predators** like Jungle cats – and Red pandas.

Fabulous pheasants

It's not just the blooms of rhododendrons that bring colour to the gloomy mountain forests. Some of the birds do too. There are more types of pheasant in the Eastern Himalayas than anywhere else in the world. The males of each type try to outdo each other – the more colourful they are, the more likely they are to attract females to mate with. By contrast, the females are dull and blend into their background so predators like hawks can't see them.

Monal pheasants shine like green metal in the sunlight and their necks glisten pink or orange depending on the angle the light rays hit them. Their feathers aren't just green-coloured; they reflect certain coloured light waves so that they add to each other in a way that makes them shine back brighter. Bright orange male Tragopan pheasants take their display one stage further by inflating metallic blue throat pouches which puff out their chests and make them look extra impressive.

As you climb higher, pine trees start to take over from the oaks and bamboo. There's no place where you can say for sure that the lowland forest stops and the highland forest starts. Sometimes they merge together. Sometimes you might find yourself in a valley with slightly more shade, or where it doesn't rain as much because the clouds have been pushed upwards by the ridges above. You'll leave lush warm jungle and find yourself in tall, dark, pine forest. Pine trees are adapted to withstand the winter snow. That Christmas tree shape lets snow slide off before its weight snaps the branches. Tough thin needle leaves are filled with antifreeze chemicals so ice can't form in their **cells** and destroy them. The waxy coating also stops water escaping – and freezing.

These cold forests are home to the world's highest-dwelling monkey. Snub-nosed monkeys live at heights of up to 4,000 metres. They have shaggy black and white fur and flat faces with nostril holes rather than noses that stick out. The big males look even odder. They have bulging pink lips.

Snub-nosed monkeys group together in bands of up to 200 and stay high in the mountain forests, even through the winter snows. At that time of the year, the leaves that they usually eat are hard to find and the monkeys eat lichen instead. Lichen is the greyish-green fuzz that grows on trees and rocks. It's a mixture of fungus and plant living together. It doesn't contain much stored energy, and Snub-nosed monkeys have specially adapted stomachs to help them get the maximum amount of nutrients from this poor food.

The biggest threat to Snub-nosed monkeys is people cutting down trees for wood to build houses and to make farmland for their sheep and cattle. This splits up their forest home into smaller and smaller pieces where it becomes harder for them to find enough food to eat. When the people want firewood, they don't always cut whole trees down. Instead they use axes to carve away half the trunks of pine trees. The wood removed is full of sticky sap that burns really easily. It's used for cooking and to heat houses over the cold winter months.

The good thing about only cutting away half the tree trunk is that the tree carries on growing next spring and summer, so in the future there'll be more firewood to gather. Also, as an added bonus, there's a type of fat, white beetle grub that eats away the open heartwood of the pine trees. The people on Kawa Karpo think these grubs are really tasty and will make long trips into the forest to hunt them out.

Paths run up and down the mountain linking the forests and the farmland with villages of wooden houses with wide roofs that look like Swiss chalets in the European Alps – the slanting roof shape is good for shedding snow in the winter. Most villages are linked up with the valleys below by roads for motor vehicles; where these end, transport is still on foot with cargo carried on ponies.

Many of the trails that cross the Himalayas are ancient trade routes. There are sections where steps have been carved into the rock, and stone bridges dating back hundreds of years. Tea from China used to be carried over the mountains into Myanmar (Burma) and then on to India. The journey took months and what had started out as green tea leaves in China arrived slightly rotten because of the fungus they carried. The people in India rather liked the taste of this tea and, when they tried it, so did many of the Chinese. Most of the tea we drink today has been allowed to age, though in more controlled conditions than on the back of a pack mule. The Chinese call it "Hong Cha" – red tea.

Explorer story:

Exploring the Yarlung Zangbo Gorge – part 1

Kintup and the coded logs

The Yarlung Zangbo in Tibet has been called the "Everest of rivers". In 240 kilometres, it drops over 3,000 metres through a series of gorges with walls 5,000 metres high in places – three times higher than the Grand Canyon in the USA. For centuries, nobody knew what lay beneath those rock walls. There were rumours of a gigantic waterfall and lost valleys. The Tibetan **Buddhists** said there were gateways to the lands where the spirits lived.

Yarlung Zangbo Gorge

C H I N A

Yarlung Zangbo

NEPAL

BHUTAN

Brahmaputra

BANGLADESH

I N D I A

BURMA

31

In 1880, Tibet was hostile territory for the British, who governed India at that time. The British sent two spies to map the river – a Tibetan monk and a tailor from Sikkim called Kintup. Kintup dressed in the flowing robes of a **pilgrim** and carried a thermometer, and a special prayer wheel in which he secretly kept a compass for finding his direction. The thermometer was to measure the temperature of boiling water which gets lower the higher up a mountain you are. Kintup would use the thermometer to work out the height, and the compass to find the direction of the peaks around him; this would help him draw maps of the area. He'd also been told to put coded marks on 500 logs and float them downstream; then other agents further down could work out if the Yarlung Zangbo led to the Brahmaputra River which flows through eastern India.

Kintup trekked further up the Yarlung Zangbo Gorge than any previous explorer, but when he went back to what he thought was the safety of a Tibetan monastery, his guide betrayed him. He was enslaved and sold to the

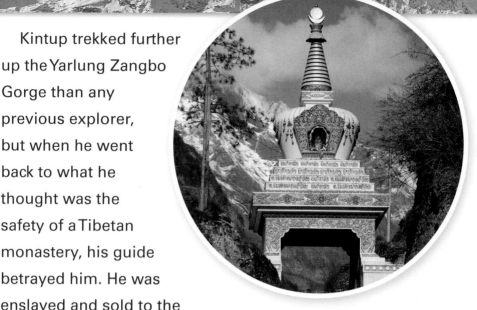

monks who lived there and put to work cleaning the monastery and growing crops for them.

Eventually, after a year, he escaped. He found someone who would take a letter back to his spymasters in India saying he still planned to float the logs down the river. Unfortunately, unknown to him, the letter was sent to the wrong people. By now, it was three years after his departure and his bosses in India presumed he was dead. Kintup launched his specially marked logs into the Yarlung Zangbo, but no one was there to find them – so still no one knew if it was the same river as the Brahmaputra. All of Kintup's work had been wasted.

Low Alpine Zone (3,500 metres)

Above the "tree line", it's too cold or windy for trees
to grow. The forest doesn't suddenly stop, but
the trees become thinner, smaller and more spaced out
the higher up the mountain you go. On windswept, open
mountainsides this will start much lower down than in
sheltered, sunlit valleys where rhododendrons and pine
trees sometimes reach right up to the high ridges. This is
called the "Alpine Zone" and it has two definite sides to
its character. In the summer, you'll find warm flower-filled
meadows backed by picture postcard snowy peaks, cows
with bells clanking under their necks and wide-roofed
timber houses.

The scenery is similar to Switzerland, except that some of the cows are humpbacked and shaggy as they have been cross-bred with mountain cattle called yaks which prefer the thin, mountain air. People come up from the villages further down the mountain, often spending the summer high up tending their cattle and sheep, and cutting the long grass to carry down to feed the animals in winter. They carry so much that they look like walking haystacks.

It's not just people taking the grass. The wildlife relies on it too. In some alpine meadows it can be hard to miss seeing a pika. Pikas are related to rabbits, but are smaller with no tail and rounder ears. They are really common, they breed quickly and their main food is grass. Overall across the Himalayas, pikas eat thousands of tonnes of grass every year. They don't hibernate in winter so they set down stores of hay in their burrows ready for when the snow covers the mountains. Pikas are really important for their **ecosystem**. Their burrowing turns over the soil, their manure helps the grass grow and they provide food for just about every predator. There are millions of pikas on the high grasslands of Tibet, and most meat-eating animals from Saker falcons to Snow leopards will prey on them if they get a chance.

One animal, the Tibetan fox, eats little else. Tibetan foxes are strange looking with square heads and long snouts. They sniff out pika burrows and sit very still until one pokes its head out. Then they pounce. With so many predators hunting them, pikas don't live longer than about 120 days.

The warm summer weather on the high slopes is only temporary. By late September, the first snow will fall and the farm animals have to be herded back down the mountainsides. If this were the Alps, these alpine meadows would be the ski slopes of the winter season. But this is the Himalayas; the **altitude** is much higher. Skiing down would be great, but the climb back up would be hard work in the low-oxygen air.

Takins

Takins look like small bison. They are in a family of mammals called goat-antelopes, related to both but not quite either. Every summer, takins move up from their forest homes to breed in the alpine meadows where there is better food to eat. Up here, small family groups join up to make massive herds hundreds strong. With so much meat on the hoof, predators like wolves and tigers move up to follow them, though on the open mountainsides with lots of eyes on the lookout, making a kill isn't easy. Even if a predator gets close, takins are bad-tempered and will often charge attackers and attempt to gore them with their horns.

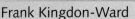

Exploring the Yarlung Zangbo Gorge – part 2

Reaching Rainbow Falls

After Kintup returned from floating his specially marked logs down the Yarlung Zangbo River, no one was keen to go back there. Everyone said it was too dangerous and, as if to prove that, an English army captain called Frederick Bailey nearly died there in 1913. He managed to walk and climb 60 kilometres up the first section, but leeches, injuries and near starvation forced him back.

Two Englishmen got further. They were Lancashire plant hunter, Frank Kingdon-Ward, and nobleman Lord Cawdor. They set off in 1924. Instead of trekking up the rocky valley, the pair climbed over the nearby mountains then descended into the gorge.

Frank Kingdon-Ward

Lord Cawdor

Following the river upstream, they climbed across the near vertical valley sides, making it past rapids and waterfalls until they could go no further. The river rumbled like thunder as it gushed out of the gap between the rock walls and tumbled 30 metres straight down. Frank Kingdon-Ward and Lord Cawdor couldn't get past Rainbow Falls. Further exploration of the Yarlung Zangbo would have to wait another 70 years until the invention of technical climbing gear and plastic kayaks.

High Alpine Zone (4,700 metres)

To the Tibetan Buddhists, the snowy white peak of Kawa Karpo is a holy place. Every year, hundreds of shaven-headed monks in long maroon-coloured robes, as well as many other people, make a **pilgrimage** around the mountain. It's a hard trek of 240 kilometres that involves crossing six high passes more than 4,800 metres high, a journey that takes several weeks. Along the way, the pilgrims dance, sing and chant prayers at holy waterfalls and peaks along the way. They hang colourful prayer flags at these places, with the belief that a prayer goes to heaven each time a flag flutters in the wind.

By now, the alpine meadows are far below. It's rockier, colder and windier here. Now there are just a few ground-hugging plants in the shelter of the rocks. These have small leathery or furry leaves which are adapted not to freeze. In the coldest, most wind-blasted places, lichens are the only thing that grow here. You see lichens on buildings in cities. In warmer, wetter areas like the forests of the lower slopes, they coat the branches in shaggy fuzz, but this high up they are more like a grey crust on the rocks.

Even in this cold and windswept area, there are animals living up here. There are insects and spiders in the thin soil that forms under the rocks and there are birds like wheatears that live on these. There are even large mammals like Bharal sheep and ibex mountain goats that have to roam vast areas to gather enough food to stay alive.

Ibex, the ultimate mountain goat

Ibex goats live on the steepest cliffs out of the reach of predators in the Western Himalayas. They show no fear of heights and are super sure-footed. In the spring, the males fight each other to mate with females, head-butting with their curved horns; then locking them together and wrestling until the weaker one gives way. It helps to have a height advantage. Each male will try to climb higher than his rival and rear up on his back legs so that he can leap with his full weight on to the other ibex. These contests often take place on the rockiest ridges and the narrowest ledges. Surprisingly few males fall to their deaths.

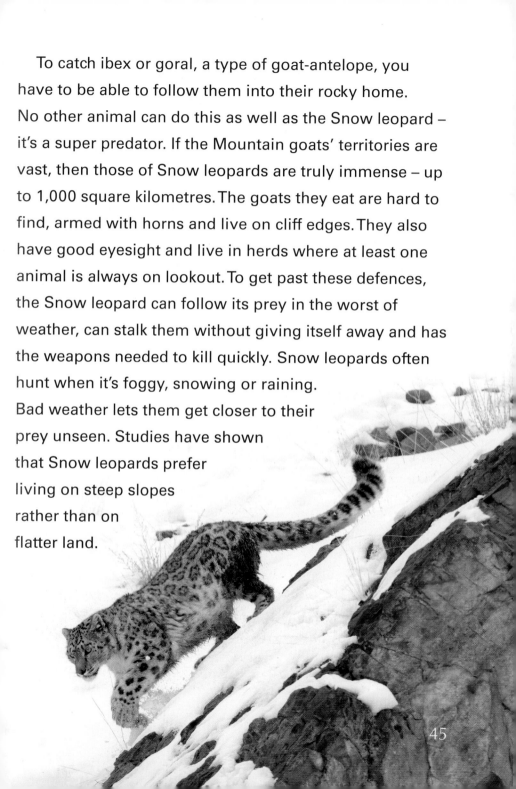

To catch ibex or goral, a type of goat-antelope, you have to be able to follow them into their rocky home. No other animal can do this as well as the Snow leopard – it's a super predator. If the Mountain goats' territories are vast, then those of Snow leopards are truly immense – up to 1,000 square kilometres. The goats they eat are hard to find, armed with horns and live on cliff edges. They also have good eyesight and live in herds where at least one animal is always on lookout. To get past these defences, the Snow leopard can follow its prey in the worst of weather, can stalk them without giving itself away and has the weapons needed to kill quickly. Snow leopards often hunt when it's foggy, snowing or raining. Bad weather lets them get closer to their prey unseen. Studies have shown that Snow leopards prefer living on steep slopes rather than on flatter land.

Here are some of the Snow leopard's amazing abilities and adaptations.

Long tail – used for balance. It can also be wrapped around the body for extra insulation like a scarf.

Wide, deep nostrils – warm up the freezing air before it gets to the lungs.

Lightly spotted greyish fur – this colouring makes it blend in against rocky backgrounds and keeps it warm in temperatures down to –40 degrees centigrade.

Large lungs – take as much oxygen as possible out of the thin air.

Sharp fangs and **retractable** claws – used for hunting.

Long hind legs – means they can spring six times their body length from a standing start. With a run up, a Snow leopard can leap 15 metres forward or six metres upwards.

This far up Kawa Karpo, Mountain goats and Snow leopards are so spread out and so shy of people that they are rarely seen. The mountain is huge and up here you feel very alone. The only sign that people ever come here are the piles of rocks and prayer flags that mark the paths. The only **domesticated** animal that can survive the cold and the thin air is the yak. Yaks have long, shaggy hair to insulate them against heat loss, and enormous lungs to take in the oxygen they need. To fit these into their chests, yaks have 15 ribs compared to the 13 in cattle, and they breathe in and out so quickly that they sound a bit like chugging trains. Yak blood has three times the number of red blood cells of normal cattle. This means they can keep going at altitudes where most animals would come to a stop – like carrying 70-kilogram loads over 5,000-metre-high mountain passes.

Tibetan farmers use yaks for just about everything. Their hair is used to make clothing, blankets and tents, and their leather is used to make shoes. Their meat is good to eat and can be stored for months. Their milk is rich in fat and makes fine cheese and butter, which is used instead of milk in Tibetan tea. For Tibetan mountain farmers, yaks have so many uses that it has been said that without yaks, people wouldn't have been able to live in the high mountain plains of Tibet.

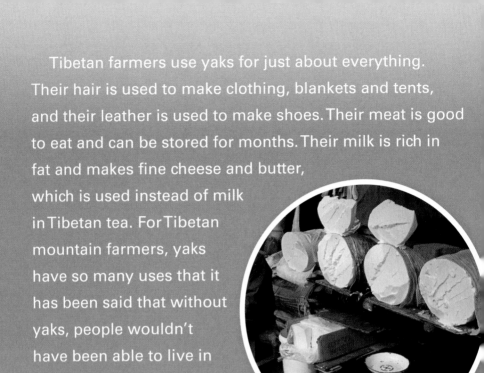

Su-Lin Young

Chinese-American explorer, Adelaide "Su-Lin"
Young, came across lots of yaks when she trekked
in the mountains close to Kawa Karpo in the 1920s.
Though the trip was part of her honeymoon, she ended
up hiking parts of it alone, with just local mountain guides
for company. She drew lots of interest from the local
Tibetan people who had not seen a lone western woman
traveller before. Su-Lin stayed in yak-hair
tents, drinking yak-butter
tea, heated over fires
burning yak dung.
She remarked
that yak hair got
everywhere,
including her
food, and she
never forgot
the smell of it.

The first giant panda cub brought from China to
the United States a few years later was named
"Su-Lin" after the Chinese-American explorer.

There are 12 million domesticated yaks in the Himalayas. They are shaggy, brownish-black or sometimes brown and white. Just about all yaks live at high levels. Fantastically adapted to mountain life they may be, but when taken to the lowlands, they give in to diseases and die. There are also still some wild yaks living in remote areas of Tibet. These are bigger – the height of a really tall man at their shoulders – and can be very fierce if approached. Most wild yaks are reddish-brown, but there's one small herd of golden-haired yaks.

Bone-smashing vultures

Riding the winds above the mountain ridges, Lammergeyer vultures search for the bodies of dead animals to scavenge. Lammergeyers specialise in eating bones. To get the bone marrow out, they carry the bones they find to great heights then drop them on to rocks, before scooping out the soft insides with their specially shaped tongues. They eat smaller bones whole. The strong acid in their stomachs dissolves them in about a day. Lammergeyers often use the same rocks for smashing their meals to pieces, and have been seen dropping tortoises on them just as they would with bones.

Exploring the Yarlung Zangbo Gorge – part 3

Kayaking

By the end of the 20th century, only a little more of the Yarlung Zangbo River Gorge had been explored since Frank Kingdon-Ward and Lord Cawdor reached Rainbow Falls in 1924. In 1993, a team with modern climbing gear had scaled the sides of Rainbow Falls but had been unable to get much further. Like the explorers before them, they decided the place was too dangerous.

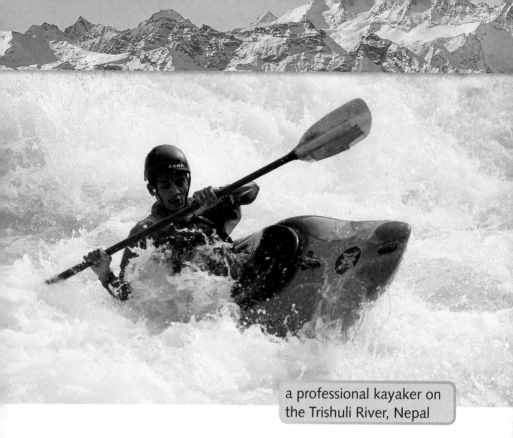

a professional kayaker on the Trishuli River, Nepal

A new plan was needed. If you couldn't climb up the Yarlung Zangbo Gorge, how about canoeing down the river from the upstream end? What was needed were strong, light kayaks and some fearless people to paddle them. The first attempt was in 1998. A team of four packed their equipment into their boats and set off into the river's rapids. But disaster soon struck. One of the overloaded kayaks flipped over and the man paddling it drowned. The team gave up their attempt and went home.

In 2002, another kayaker, called Scott Lindgren, was planning to explore the Yarlung Zangbo. He liked the other team's plan but thought that their boats had been too heavy. He decided to keep his team's seven kayaks light and to hire lots of local men to carry all of their food and camping gear. The expedition set off at the end of the winter when the temperatures were freezing and snow still lay thick on the ground. This was not as foolish as it seems. Lindgren chose this time of year as it was long after the summer monsoon rains and before the snow melted in the spring. This meant the river would be running at its lowest for the year. Still, the rapids were fearsome. Some places were giant cauldrons where the water whirlpooled around enormous boulders, and there were sudden drops where the boats would go right under. Lindgren and his team wore dry suits and were sealed into their kayaks with waterproof "spray decks" so that when they flipped over they could roll back upright. Their rule was never to exit their boats. They knew they would get washed away, smashed on rocks or freeze to death in the icy water if they did.

The parts of the gorge they were kayaking, some believed, had not been seen by people before. In places, the river had changed direction where landslides had blocked the valley. The kayakers paddled their boats past valley sides where goat-antelope gorals grazed. They saw the trails left by migrating takins and, at one river bend, they found the tracks of a leopard mother and her cub.

Finally, 14 days in, the kayakers had to stop as the river was just too dangerous. They were near Rainbow Falls and to carry on would have meant certain death. Lindgren made the decision that the whole expedition would carry on overland through dense forest, and then up and around a snowy mountain ridge.

The porters carried the food, and the kayakers put straps on their boats so that they looked like long colourful rucksacks. This was the toughest bit of the trip. Even the normally fearless kayakers admitted that half climbing, half sliding across the mountain was the most dangerous part. When they got back to the river, they found it was twice as big and doubly dangerous now that another river had joined it. They rode a few more rapids; then all agreed that the "lower gorge" would have to wait. For now, that part of the Yarlung Zangbo had knocked back yet more explorers.

Above the snow line (5,500 metres)

Sherpas are the experts of Himalayan mountain climbing. They are the people that mountaineers want to have with them if they wish to climb the highest summits. Originally Sherpas lived in Eastern Nepal, and their name means "east people". Sherpas gained a reputation for being incredibly strong carriers of supplies due to their hiking abilities, strength and comfort with altitude. In 1953, Sherpa Tenzing Norgay was the first to climb the highest mountain on Earth, Mount Everest. He climbed with Edmund Hillary from New Zealand. Apa Sherpa climbed Everest 21 times. Since then, Kami Rita Sherpa has summited Everest 26 times. Many Sherpas have completed their own expeditions, like the team of three women who summited K2 in 2014. Nirmal Purja, a mountaineer from Nepal, currently holds the world record for climbing 14 of the world's highest peaks in just over six months.

wind carries snow

cornice

This close to the Himalayan peaks, snow and ice cover the steep slopes. On the highest ridges, the wind blows the snow into shapes like ocean waves called "cornices". Some of these overhang cliff edges. They can fall off without warning, as **avalanches** that tumble down the mountainside, smashing everything in their way. Snow builds up in the valleys – squashed hard, it flows a few metres downhill every day in rivers of ice called "glaciers". Crossing glaciers on foot is dangerous. There can be huge cracks in the ice hidden under the snow, known as "crevasses". Climbers have to stay roped together so that they can save anyone who falls into these.

As for life, little can survive up here. The temperature rarely rises above freezing and the air is too thin. You are above the clouds now and the sky looks darker blue as you are closer to outer space. The sunlight is bright and getting badly sunburnt can be a real problem. Added to that, the wind whips tiny ice crystals across your eyeballs. Unless you wear tinted goggles or sunglasses with sidepieces, you risk snow blindness. This is when the surface of your eyes gets so irritated by wind, ice crystals and sunlight that your eyes water all the time. Opening them is painful. You see nothing but tears. Keeping them closed is just as bad. All you can do is rest your eyes – for days, if necessary – and wait for them to get better.

What's worse – you are approaching the "Death Zone".

The Death Zone

Seven kilometres above sea level, humans can't survive for long. There's simply not enough oxygen in the air.

The effects of lack of oxygen are noticeable at only 2,500 metres, which is about twice the height of Ben Nevis – Britain's highest mountain. You get out of breath quickly. Getting to sleep is difficult. People often suffer from headaches. This is called "mild altitude sickness" and isn't dangerous provided that you don't run around or do too much exercise. After a week or two, the body gets used to the altitude by making more red blood cells to carry oxygen to the muscles. This is called "acclimatising".

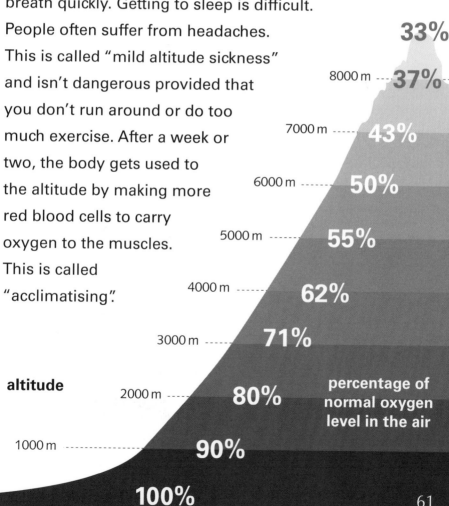

33%

8000 m ---- 37%

7000 m ---- 43%

6000 m ---- 50%

5000 m ---- 55%

4000 m ---- 62%

3000 m ---- 71%

altitude

2000 m ---- 80%

percentage of normal oxygen level in the air

1000 m ---- 90%

100%

There are, however, some far more serious problems that can start above 3,600 metres. Occasionally, the lungs can fill with fluid or the brain can swell. Both of these conditions can kill quickly. People with them must be taken to low altitude. They must get medical help.

Amazingly, there are some animals that do well this high up. Tiny jumping spiders have been found 6,700 metres up Mount Everest. They live under rocks, darting out to snatch up flies that have been blown up the mountain by the strong winds.

Even higher up are Bar-headed geese that actually fly right over Mount Everest. Every winter, they fly from Tibet to fields and wetlands in India where there is more food to eat. To do this, they have to fly across the Himalayas. Beating their wings quickly keeps them warm and helps get oxygen to their muscles. They fly very quickly, boosted by the wind. Bar-headed geese probably started flying this migration route millions of years ago when the Himalayas were much lower.

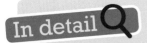

The day the sky fell on Everest

On 10 May 1996, the weather was calm when several groups of mountaineers started their climb up Mount Everest. Around 4 o'clock in the afternoon, the wind started to get up as two **"jet stream"** winds collided, pulling air away from the peak. The effect was like raising the height of the mountain by another 500 metres. It put a normally safe part of the mountain into the "Death Zone". The unusual effect only lasted a couple of hours but that was enough to kill eight climbers.

The lack of oxygen is the reason why there are no human settlements above 6,000 metres. Most climbers who scale the tallest mountains carry oxygen tanks. However, people have climbed Everest without them. Reinhold Messner did it twice!

Even with extra oxygen, climbers can't afford to stay for long on Himalayan mountain peaks. Tiredness from the climb up takes its toll and so does the intense cold. Going down can be the most dangerous part – this is when mountaineers make mistakes, like failing to clip on to their ropes properly, and end up falling hundreds of metres to their deaths. There are bodies still frozen in the snows of Everest and K2. It's too hard and too expensive to go back and recover them.

Lost gloves

Maurice Herzog was a French mountaineer. In 1950, he'd just become the first person to reach the summit of Annapurna in Nepal. He was overjoyed but also overtired. He took his gloves off to get something out of his rucksack. They slid away down an icy slope and out of view. He was so tired, he forgot he had a spare pair of socks in his rucksack, which he could have put on his hands. By now Maurice could see his climbing partner was far ahead. He was worried he was being left behind. So, he clambered down to his base camp with his hands bare. Maurice had long lost any feeling in his fingers when he finally arrived. They were blotched violet and white and had frozen solid.

His team-mates spent most of the night rubbing his hands to try and get blood flowing in them. They did the same with his toes which were also frostbitten. But, when parts of the human body freeze solid, the tiny cells that they are made up of are destroyed. Maurice had to have most of his fingers removed when he made it off the mountain. Both Maurice and his climbing partner lost all of their toes.

The Yeti

In 1951, the world's press was buzzing with the latest photographs taken on Mount Everest by British climber Eric Shipton. They appeared to show the footprints of a giant human walking on two feet across the snow. People said the tracks could belong to the "Yeti", which was shown in pictures in Tibetan temples. There were also reports of sightings by several climbers of what had looked like gigantic shaggy ape-men. Reinhold Messner even claimed to have met Yetis at close range, though he has since said – like other witnesses – that the sightings were probably of the almost unknown **Tibetan blue bear**.

So far, there's been no hard evidence to show that a hairy ape-man inhabits the Himalayas. There are no photographs, and all the fur and skin samples that have been tested have been shown to belong to other animals – usually bears. So does the Yeti exist? Who knows? The Government of Bhutan in the central Himalayas certainly thinks so. It has set up a nature reserve that stretches from the rhododendron forests up to the high peaks, in the hope that the Yeti may yet show up.

Growing mountains

Not all of the high peaks of the Himalayas are covered with ice and snow. There are places where winds have blasted it away, leaving bare rock. If you look carefully at this rock, you can find fossils of coiled shells called ammonites that once contained squid-like animals. Ammonites lived at the same time as the dinosaurs and died out at the same time as they did, 65 million years ago. Ammonites lived in the sea. So how did they get kilometres up the biggest mountains in the world? The answer is **plate tectonics** and is the reason the Himalayas formed.

Earth's outer **crust** is made of separate pieces called **tectonic plates**. These float on top of a layer of the earth called the **mantle**. The mantle is hot and contains **molten** rock. Over long periods of time, the rock in the mantle moves around and this slowly pushes the tectonic plates. They only move a few centimetres every year but over millions of years this means that whole continents can move thousands of kilometres.

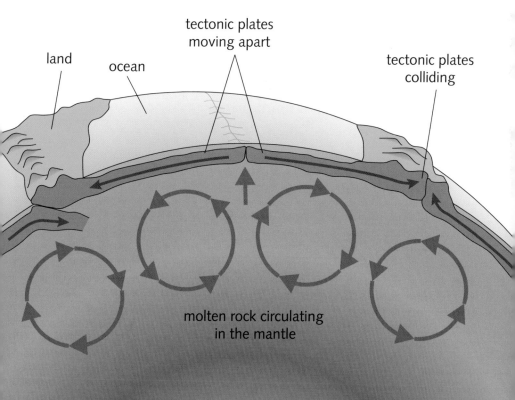

tectonic plates
moving apart

land

ocean

tectonic plates
colliding

molten rock circulating
in the mantle

Earth's core

65 million years ago, the tectonic plate that India sits on was much further southwest from where it is now. There was a sea in the space between India and the main part of Asia. That is where the ammonites lived. When the ammonites died, they sank to the bottom of the sea. Over the years, layers of sand and mud piled on top of them. As layer upon layer built up, the sand and mud was squashed and eventually formed into rock.

Long after that – around 50 million years ago – the Indian plate started moving towards Asia. As it crashed into it, it started pushing the land up. The Himalayas are called "fold" mountains. In places, the mountains look like they have been made of a giant piece of clay that's been squashed up. Here, the layers of rock stay together and fold. What once were flat layers of mud and sand at the bottom of the sea are now sitting upright. Sometimes this folded rock splits into gigantic cracks called "faults". One side slips down leaving jagged rocks sticking upwards out of the surface.

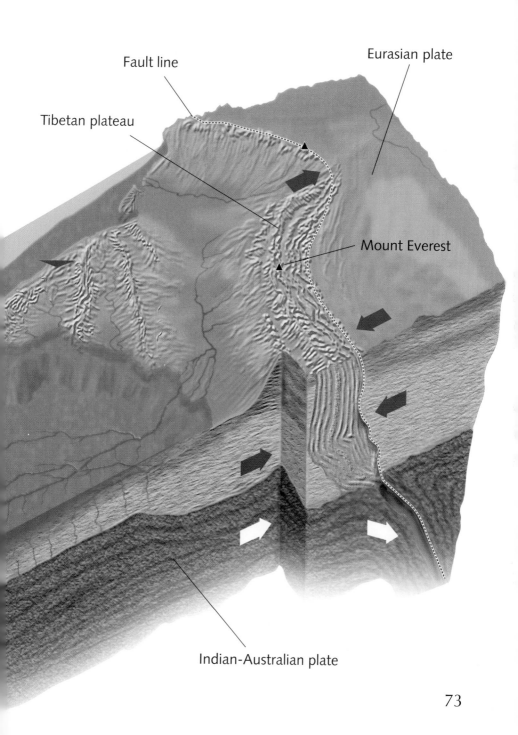

Fault line

Eurasian plate

Tibetan plateau

Mount Everest

Indian-Australian plate

73

Sometimes the tectonic plates of Earth's crust get stuck together. The movements in the mantle underneath them are still trying to push them but there's no movement. The force keeps building up. It can build up for years and on the surface, there's no sign that anything is wrong. Suddenly, without warning, the tectonic plates jolt free. Shock waves speed out in all directions, shaking the land from side to side and up and down. These are earthquakes.

earthquake damage to buildings in a village near Kathmandu

The Indian tectonic plate is moving into Asia at a speed of around three centimetres each year and, although that seems tiny, this has been going on for nearly 50 million years. The forces involved are massive. The layered rocks of the Himalayas were once mud and sand on the ocean floor. Now they are on the roof of the world and this is still rising by over six centimetres every year. The mightiest mountains on the planet are getting even bigger!

Glossary

altitude	how high up something is above sea level
avalanches	snow sliding down the mountain, often when snowfall has been heavy
Buddhists	people who follow an Asian religion called Buddhism; many Tibetans are Buddhists
cells	the "building blocks" that make up all living things
climate	weather conditions
crust	the outer rock layer of the earth
crystals	regular-sided pieces of ice or mineral
digestive systems	the organs in animals' bodies, like the stomach and the intestines, that break down food and take nutrients out of it
domesticated	animals bred and looked after by people, like dogs, cattle and yaks
ecosystem	a whole, natural habitat including all the animals and plants that live there
equator	imaginary line around the middle of the earth that divides the Northern and Southern Hemispheres
gorges	valleys with steep or vertical, rocky sides
jet stream	a very fast wind in the upper atmosphere, a layer of air that surrounds the earth
lichen	fuzzy or crusty, light-green mixture of plants and fungus that grows on tree branches and rocks
mantle	the hotter layer of the earth underneath the crust
molten	turned liquid by heat
nutrients	substances that help plants and animals grow
pilgrim	a person travelling to a holy place to pray
pilgrimage	a trip taken to visit a holy place
plate tectonics	a theory to explain the movement of continents

pollinate	when the wind or animals pass pollen from the flowers of one plant to another which leads to them making seeds
predators	animals, like Snow leopards, that eat other animals
retractable	can be pulled back when not being used, like the claws of a Snow leopard and most other cats
tectonic plates	the parts of the earth's crust (outer layer) that make up the continents – tectonic plates sit on top of the mantle
Tibetan blue bear	a large and almost unknown type of bear that may be the cause of the stories about the Yeti

Index

Mountain zones

High Alpine Zone

Low Alpine Zone

Temperate Zone

Subtropical Zone

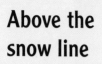
Above the snow line

5,500 m

4,700 m

3,500 m

1,500 m

 Ideas for reading

Written by Clare Dowdall, PhD
Lecturer and Primary Literacy Consultant

Reading objectives:
- ask questions to improve their understanding
- summarise the main ideas drawn from more than one paragraph, identifying key details that support the main ideas
- explain and discuss their understanding of what they have read, including through formal presentations and debates, maintaining a focus on the topic and using notes where necessary

Spoken language objectives:
- ask relevant questions to extend their understanding and knowledge
- participate in discussions, presentations, performances, role play, improvisations and debates

Curriculum links: Geography – climate zones

Resources: whiteboards or notebooks and pens, ICT for research, paper and pens/ ICT for preparing an advert.

Build a context for reading
- Explain that you will be reading about the mountain range called the Himalayas.
- Collect any known information about the Himalayas.
- Read the blurb. Ask children to suggest what types of climate, vegetation and wildlife might be found at different levels of the mountain range.

Understand and apply reading strategies
- Turn to the contents. Discuss how focusing on the contents can help as we prepare for reading (information can be deduced to help build a context; connections to existing knowledge can be made).
- In pairs, ask children to use the contents to note questions to guide their reading about a zone of their choice on a whiteboard. Share the questions raised.